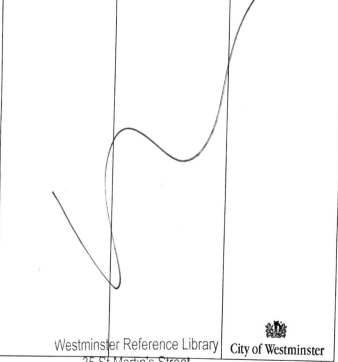

For Toby and Leon, dearest friends,
especially because this is about films

791.43028

Ds

LIBRARY OF CONGRESS CATALOGING IN PUBLICATION DATA
Miklowitz, Gloria D   Movie stunts and the people who do them.
Includes index.   1. Stunt men and women—Juvenile literature. I. Title.
PN1995.9.S7M5   791.43'028'0922   80-7984   ISBN 0-15-256038-6   ISBN 0-15-256039-4 (pbk.)

First edition

B C D E

CONTENTS

THE FIRST STUNT PEOPLE

The scene on the screen begins pleasantly. We see the plush dining room on the luxury cruise ship *Poseidon*. At one end of the room a band plays on a raised platform. Over the dance floor a large glass skylight floods the room with light. Tables bulge with rich foods and fine wines. People eat, talk quietly, laugh, dance.

And then disaster.

An explosion!

In the sudden silence those on the dance floor freeze, their eyes raised in questioning alarm toward the sound. Diners grip the table edges, gasp, turn puzzled looks toward each other. The band strikes up a lively tune, loud in the stillness.

Above the music come the other sounds. Creaking, straining, groaning, as if the steel girders of the giant floating hotel were alive and in great pain.

Passengers on the S.S. *Poseidon* as water
breaks through into the Grand Salon
(*The Poseidon Adventure*. Courtesy of Twentieth Century-
Fox. Copyright © 1972 Twentieth Century-Fox Film Corp.)

Now starts the slow, slow, agonizing roll-over as the ship, like a wounded animal, turns deck down to the sea bottom. Men and women slide from their seats, skid crazily up the walls, are smashed by flying dinner plates, silver, musical instruments, chairs. Lights dim. There are screams, terrible, frightened cries, the sound of rushing water, thuds, shrieks.

Only moments before the skylight was above the dance floor; now it is below. The dining tables, fixed to the ballroom floor, are now upside down, hanging from above. And clutching the edges of those tables, dangling by their fingers, are eleven desperate passengers. How long can they hold on before they must let go?

We sit there in the theater with dry mouths, eyes wide, hearts pounding. One by one the people drop, arms flailing, screams echoing as they plunge to the ceiling below. One man suffers a fate worse than the others. He crashes, back down, through the glass skylight, landing—who knows where.

In those few dramatic moments we believe everything we see. We believe that men and women are drowning, being crushed, and are falling great distances to their deaths. When we leave the theater, we feel relieved and satisfied. For ninety minutes we have escaped into other lives, experienced the horror of *The Poseidon Adventure* without having to go through it ourselves. For a moment we may wonder. Those action scenes were so real, did they truly happen? Is it possible real people fell to the deck below? Really jumped into the burning sea? Really drowned?

Yes—and no.

Yes. The people we saw on the screen really did slide along the floor, get hit by objects, fall, really dive into a flaming sea.

But no. They did not get hurt. No one drowned.

The men and women who perform the daring and often dangerous action that is part of almost every television and motion-picture story today are special people. They are professional stunt men and women. They know precisely what they are doing and how to do it. Most are extraordinary athletes with the grace and timing of dancers. They plan ahead what they must do. And they have no intention of getting hurt, although sometimes they do.

Stunt men and women usually double for movie and TV stars. That means they perform the dangerous action we think the stars are actually doing. When we see *Wonder Woman,* we think it is the star, Linda Carter, who is running along the edge of the rooftop and jumps to the top of the moving car. It isn't. It's Jeannie Epper, Linda's stunt double. They are almost the same height and body build. Jeannie can be made up to look like Linda. And in a scene in which the difference might be noticed, the camera focuses away from Jeannie's face, or she turns her head.

Sometimes stunt people are also actors. A stunt man may play a Japanese soldier who is shot out of a high tower to the jungle floor. A stunt woman may portray a pioneer mother who must control a team of runaway horses.

The reason stunt people are needed is simple. A film often depends on the presence of the star. If the star is out sick or injured, filming stops. The cameramen, the lighting people, and all the others hired for making that film must be paid even though they aren't working. So, rather than risk the star, a double is called in to do the dangerous action.

Paul Stader, who has doubled for Cary Grant and Johnny Weissmuller (as Tarzan), was called to double for Ryan O'Neal in *What's Up Doc?* The scene called for Ryan to drive a VW off a dock at full speed, toward a moving ferry. The car was to fall short and land in the water, then sink slowly. Stader was to drive the car into the water; then there would be a cut. The next thing the viewer would see was Barbra Streisand and Ryan O'Neal swimming away from the sinking car.

The stunt seemed simple enough, except it didn't work quite as planned. When Stader landed in the water, the windshield broke and the car quickly filled and sank. It took Stader, a champion swimmer and diver, two minutes to make it to the surface. He almost didn't. If Ryan O'Neal had been at the wheel, it's certain he would have died.

What is stunting?

It is spectacular entertainment involving a certain amount of risk to the performer. It is entirely visual. More important, it must be action which takes place within a story. Its purpose is to further the drama of which it is only a part.

When Karl Wallenda, the famous aerialist, took a 1,000-foot-long walk on a high wire about 700 feet above a deep gorge, it was not stunting. The event was spectacular. It involved danger. It was entirely visual and was intended to entertain. But the walk was not part of a drama in which Wallenda was playing a part.

Stunting, as we know it, began with movies. But a version of it has existed since classical times. Drawings from 4,000 years ago on the island of Crete, near Greece, show young men somersaulting over the backs of charging bulls during religious celebrations.

Roman gladiators, usually prisoners or slaves, were an early version of stunt men. They were trained to become expert chariot drivers, superb horsemen, and first-rate swordsmen. In the arenas they performed for audiences of 20,000 people or more. Their purpose was to entertain. Unfortunately the gladiators were not "acting," as today's stunt men are. Their performances were life-and-death struggles against wild animals or others as skilled as they. If they did not lose their lives, they were often severely injured.

In A.D. 44 the emperor Claudius ordered the staging of an unusual drama. The players were to act out the capture and destruction of an entire town and the surrender of its leaders.

Today a play is "pretend." Claudius's play was for real. The actors, dressed as Roman soldiers, galloped into the set, a town built for the purposes. While a large audience sat nearby, the actors set fire to the houses, rode down and butchered women and children, and battled to the death any who resisted. The people who performed in the play were gladiators. They used all their skills and ingenuity to put on a good show and survive. Many did not.

It wasn't until Shakespeare's time in England that stunting in its present form began. The fights in *Hamlet, Romeo and Juliet,* and *Macbeth* were really fights, but no one was meant to be hurt. Skill was required of the actors, and risk was involved, but the scenes were staged.

Stunting in the theater for the next years included battles and sieges and elaborate fights onstage. In 1899 the play *Ben Hur,* about Roman times, was put on in England. Only eight cities had large enough theaters to hold the many performers in the huge production. In the famous chariot race, a team of horses galloped on a treadmill. Behind the horses the scenery flashed by, giving the illusion of movement.

The stage was confining. Horses couldn't gallop freely in so small a space. With the invention of moving pictures, action could take place anywhere a camera's eye could record.

Early films were silent with some subtitles to tell what was going on. The audience figured out what was happening not through what was said in subtitles, but from the action on the screen. Action held interest. Because of this, stunt people came into their own.

The actors and actresses who played in early films did their own stunts. Pearl White, star in many episodes of *The Perils of Pauline* (1914), and Helen Gibson, who played Helen in *The Hazards of Helen* (1914), often did very dangerous things. Gibson did a motorcycle stunt in one short film which was as risky as anything done today. Traveling at full speed, she chased after a runaway freight train. She rode through a wooden gate, shattering it completely, up a station platform, and through the open doors of a boxcar on a siding. Her motorcycle continued traveling through the air until it landed on a flatcar of a passing train.

In 1916 she was badly hurt when she fell between a team of galloping horses. It was only one of many injuries she received during her career. Being hurt became routine for stars doing their own stunts.

The early stars usually didn't use doubles until they were injured. Pearl White hurt her back badly filming one of the *Pauline* episodes. In 1923 John Stevenson was killed doubling for her in the film *Plunder*. Dressed in female costume and blonde wig, he jumped from a moving bus onto the steel girders of a bridge as the bus passed below him. When he leaped from the top of the bus, he failed to get a good hold on the girder and fell. He died a few hours later of head injuries.

Payment for dangerous stunts in those early films was very low. In 1916, during the filming of *Intolerance,* 2,000 extras were hired. Many of them were actually doing stunt work. During the shooting of one scene 67 people suffered injuries. These extras were paid only $1.25 a day plus carfare and free lunch. In those days $7 a week bought the barest living.

The star who performed his own stunts did better. Helen Gibson earned $50 a week in *The Hazards of Helen,* and later her salary went up to $450 a week. Pearl White was paid $250 a week for *The Perils of Pauline.* But Bobby Dunn, a member of the Mack Sennett team in the early days of movies, earned only $5 for a very difficult stunt. He dived off the roof of a Los Angeles hotel, falling 80 feet into a nine-by-five-foot tank of water which was only five feet deep. Dunn had already lost an eye in a similar stunt.

Some of the early stunt people seemed to ignore the dangers of their work. They climbed buildings, holding onto rusted drainpipes, ignoring the fact that if they fell, they'd hit the concrete below.

Harold Lloyd and Buster Keaton, famous stunt actors who were also their own directors, started a new approach to stunting. There was no virtue in danger for its own sake, they said. Why be foolhardy when a little preparation for a stunt could lessen its danger?

If there was a fall from a high building, for example, they planned ways to make the landing less dangerous. When they dug a hole in the ground, filled it with straw, and covered it with dirt, the fall was softened. Even so, there was plenty of danger. Keaton fell from the second floor of a building during the filming of *One Week* in 1920. He damaged both elbows and his back, despite preparation of the ground below.

Early actors taught the new stunt people two things. They stressed the need for great physical skill, and they emphasized the importance of careful, exacting preparation.

Keaton taught himself back somersaults, butterflies, and flip-flaps in order to perfect body control. Stunts were tried out before filming so problems could be caught and ironed out. If there was to be a fight scene, it was planned as carefully as a dance. Each actor knew where he should be and what he should do to whom at each moment.

No matter how careful the planning, mistakes happened. Keaton had carefully worked out a stunt which involved his leaping from the top of a moving train to grab a rope dangling from a water tower. The rope was to release a jet of water which would soak Keaton and make everyone laugh. It all figured out well on paper. But during the filming, when Keaton grabbed the rope, it released so much water that it threw him backwards. He fell with the back of his neck across a metal rail and broke his neck.

Early stunt people were often courageous to the point of being foolhardy. This was caused by the audience's always expecting new, more daring stunts. Viewers wanted falls from greater heights, leaps from faster trains, stunts they hadn't seen before.

Eventually the difficulty of the stunt became greater than the ability of the actor to do it. With film budgets increasing, a need to protect the main actors from injury grew. If the leading player was out, hundreds of other people couldn't work. More and more, specialists were called in to do the hard action work. Pilots who could fly and do stunts found work in the movies. Circus people, cowboys, athletes, men and women with special skills began to be in demand. These were the people who created the new job of stunt person in the movies.

PREPARING FOR A STUNT

In the film *Highpoint*, we see Christopher Plummer, one of the stars, being chased around the roof of a restaurant. The restaurant is at the top of the world's tallest building, 117 stories above the ground. Suddenly Plummer loses his balance. We see him dropping, arms and legs kicking, to certain death.

Is it really Christopher Plummer? If it isn't, who is it, and will he survive?

Doubling for Plummer was Dar Robinson, doing "one of the scariest jumps I ever attempted." In the finished film we see him falling for six heart-stopping seconds and "assume" he smashes to the ground. Of course, he doesn't. Diving streetward at 102 mph, Robinson fell about 800 feet. Then, only 300 to 350 feet from the ground, he opened a hidden parachute. The fall was slowed, and the landing, though hard, broke no bones.

Robinson's fall cost $250,000 to film. It's rumored he received $100,000 for doing it. Eight cameras, including one in a helicopter, were set up to cover him. The planning by Robinson before doing the stunt was enormous. Yet the scene appeared for only five seconds on the screen.

When he leaped, it took six seconds into the fall before he had enough air resistance to begin adjusting his body position. As he fell, he counted the

Dar Robinson free-
falling in the movie *Highpoint*
(Photo by John Giannini and Alan Markfield)

seconds—1001, 1002, etc. At 1006, he reached in to pull the chute, taking one more second. Would the chute open? Two seconds later he was floating down. When he landed, he lay there for a moment, thinking, *Wow! Boy! Was that ever something!* This time everything had gone right. If the parachute hadn't worked ... but it had. And the wind hadn't driven him into the trees. All the planning had paid off.

No good stunt person does a "gag" without careful planning. Every possible danger must be considered for even the simplest fall. Hal Needham tells of several weeks' work before performing an airplane/horse stunt for the cameras. In the scene a man was to jump from the wing of a moving airplane onto the back of a man on a galloping horse.

First, a plane which could be flown slowly with absolute control had to be selected. Then a horse had to be trained to run without spooking because of the plane flying so closely above it. To keep the aircraft under control, the pilot had to retain a nose-up attitude. This meant he couldn't see the direction the horse took on the ground. Needham navigated from the wing of the moving aircraft, shouting directions to the pilot. Coordination among pilot, Needham, and the stunt man on the horse required several weeks of rehearsal. On the screen the action looked easy.

Often accidents happen just because enough planning isn't done. Stephanie Epper says she learned that lesson the hard way. During most of thirteen years she doubled for Amanda Blake on *Gunsmoke*. Horse falls, driving four-ups (wagons pulled by four horses), fights—all were routine for her. She has been knocked down by cars and dropped from helicopters into the sea, all movie stunts. But "the closest call" Stephanie remembers came about because she herself didn't check out the stunt.

The scene called for Stephanie, dressed in evening gown and high heels, to drive in a jeep with two men. The jeep would be traveling at 45 mph over rough ground and high grass. The stunt men in the car said they'd examined the ground the jeep would ride over, and it looked okay. They were careful stunt men. Stephanie believed them.

During the stunt, however, the jeep traveled about ten feet farther than planned. Speeding through high grass on very hard ground, it hit a rock. Stephanie was flipped out and wound up with a deep gash on her leg. It was lucky she hadn't landed on her head. "Next time," she says, "I'll do my own checking."

Terry Leonard, stunt coordinator for the film *Apocalypse Now,* tells of planning one difficult stunt for five days. He and another stunt man played enemy sentries in the film. They had to fall from a sixty-eight-foot-high bamboo tower when it exploded. The tower was fixed to an old bombed-out bridge and held together with fiber. It resembled a too-tall Tinker Toy. Below was the river, studded with jagged parts from the former bridge.

When the tower was constructed, no thought was given to how the stunt men would manage. Leonard and his co-stunt man spent many hours underwater, groping around in the muddy depths. They wanted to pinpoint as many dangerous projections as possible and remove those they could. Eventually they cleared a ten-foot-square area into which they hoped to land.

When the tower exploded, the stunt men were expected to ride it down into the river. Not only would they have to avoid landing on any of the obstructions, but worse, they had to fall into shallow water. The river varied in depth during the day. By the time they were ready to go, it was a sixty-eight-foot drop into *five feet of water.* If they didn't smack flat, they'd hit bottom.

Timing was critical, too. The tower would blow on the fifth explosion. The special effects people were using an explosive which went off very fast and caused a tremendous concussion. Leonard had to act as if he had no idea the tower would blow up while he had to count the fast-paced explosions so he could jump instantly on the fifth one.

"When those bomb pots blow you off," he said, "no matter how you're going—backwards, sideways, flipping, or twisting—you have to come out of it and hit flat." And while you wait for the right explosion, "your old heart starts pounding pretty hard." He knew there was no calling it off at the last minute. He had to go, ready or not, and do it right the first time because it would take too long to rebuild the tower for a second take.

The scene was taken in two camera angles. One showed the men being blown off the tower. The other showed the tower coming down "like twenty-seven hundred boxes of Ohio strike-'em-on-the-seat-of-the-pants matches."

Falling through the black smoke, Leonard suddenly remembered he had better turn onto his back. Only twenty feet above the water he flipped over and went into a static position. He hit the water flat and sank no more than six inches. Leonard's body took a pretty hard pounding. Falling sixty-eight feet onto your back in water hurts plenty. For several days after, he was spitting up blood.

No matter how careful the planning, things do go wrong. In the film *The Jerk* Debbie Evans learned a lesson she will not soon forget.

The gag was to drive a motorcycle through a burning barricade. It looked easy, almost routine. Before doing it, she went over the setup with the stunt coordinator.

The barricade Debbie was to drive through seemed to be made properly. The wood was thin; it would break easily. True, it would be on fire when Debbie motorcycled through it. But she would be wearing a fire-retardant suit made of Nomex. Her chest, her head, and part of her back were protected. "No need to cover your arms," the coordinator said. "It'll be easy. No problem."

Debbie revved up her motorcycle, lined herself up, and drove full speed into the burning barricade. That's when things began going wrong.

The wood, though thin, didn't break away as it was supposed to. Only part of it gave way; most of it bent forward. Burning chips clung to Debbie, sticking to her bare arms. She had to fall off her motorcycle to put out the embers.

The wood should have been scored or weakened, she realized later. If it had been, she wouldn't have been slowed going through. She wouldn't have collected so many pieces of burning wood. More important, she should have asked about the fuel used for the fire. In place of gasoline, the special effects man had used diesel fuel, which is an oil. It's sticky. The burning wood chips stuck to Debbie, instead of flying off.

Debbie, like Stephanie, had learned an important lesson that day. When your own life is at stake, you can't be too careful. In the future she would check and double-check any stunt she was asked to do.

Few people watching a movie realize how much planning goes into the action scenes. Stunt people are becoming more and more involved in planning and setting up their own stunts. "Please place that camera farther away," a stunt person may say. "If I jump from that horse, I might land on the camera." Or, "Since I'll be wearing a long dress, anyway, would it matter if I wore low-heeled shoes? It would be safer for me than heels when I have to run around that roof ledge and jump to the ground below."

Fred Waugh, one of Hollywood's top stunt men, analyzes each stunt to take as much of the gamble out of it as possible. When working in *Spider Man*, Waugh had to crawl along the face of a building fourteen stories above ground. As he searched for toe- and fingerholds, viewers gasped. How could anyone take such a chance? But Waugh had figured out the stunt in advance.

He wore a body harness with a cable manned by seven men. The cable was attached to a belt-and-swivel arrangement so that the invisible wires, controlled by the men, would help keep his body flat against the building.

Many stunt people even require their own safety crews to work with them. These experts can spot trouble before it happens and rush in to save the stunt person. Paul Stader gives a good example of this.

When he drove the VW car off the dock in *What's Up Doc?* scuba divers, strangers to him, stood by in case anything went wrong. The car sank. Stader was wearing a Japanese kimono when doubling for Ryan O'Neal. He was caught at the bottom of the bay, unable to escape from the side windows because of heavy silt which poured in. When he tried to swim through the broken windshield, he cut his hands, and the kimono caught on the jagged glass. Precious seconds were lost while he struggled to free himself. Starving for oxygen, he finally popped to the surface two minutes later. Where were the scuba divers, his safety men? Staring at the spot where the VW had gone down. When Stader appeared, they took off, knowing they'd better not show up again. Stader never will do a stunt without his own safety crew.

Bob Yerkes, stunt man, explains how he helps friends prepare for difficult stunts. Beth Newfer turned to Yerkes when she was asked to double in *Wonder Woman.* "We want you to leap from the ground up to an open second-story window," she was told. Newfer wasn't sure how she'd do it but remembered Bob Yerkes's expertise.

In the Clyde Beatty circus for many years he was an expert acrobat and trampoline performer. Beth knew he'd taught people to do triple somersaults from high trapezes. Maybe he could help her.

Yerkes's backyard in Northridge, California, resembles a small circus. There's a trapeze set with net below, a cannon, exercise bars, a trampoline, and other equipment.

Yerkes said there were several ways to do the stunt. The leap up to the second-story window could actually be a jump down, backwards. Then the film could be reversed. If you've ever seen a person dive into a pool, then watched as the film reversed, you get the idea.

The trouble was that sometimes the stunt looked faked that way.

Another way to do it would be to use a catapult to rocket Beth to the higher level. But the scene didn't call for her to travel through the air for any distance, the main reason for using a catapult.

Yerkes solved the problem this way. He hung a pedestal board at the height of the window ledge. Then, on the ground, some distance away, he set up a teeterboard. His plan was to jump from the pedestal board to the teeterboard. This would throw Beth upward. But how could Beth's flight be accurate enough to land her on the board Yerkes had just left? Her weight, the distance the teeterboard was placed from the pedestal, the force Yerkes exerted when he landed—all had to be figured. During these trial-and-error jumps Beth wore a safety belt around her waist. If she missed the landing, she could be let down to the ground easily.

Beth and Yerkes practiced the stunt again and again. When they were sure the teeterboard was set at the right distance from the landing and Beth could do the stunt well, they were ready.

At the movie studio they set up the teeterboard exactly as it had been in Yerkes's backyard. Yerkes jumped from the two-story high window, instead of the pedestal board. Beth flew up, just like Wonder Woman, and landed precisely where she should have. When the film was cut, it didn't show Yerkes jumping to the teeterboard. In fact, the teeterboard didn't appear at all on the screen. The scene showed the real Wonder Woman, hands raised and ready to leap. Then we saw Beth, dressed as Wonder Woman, flying through the air and landing on the ledge. Then there was a close-up of the real Wonder Woman again, looking as if she had just landed.

Nobody expresses the importance of careful planning better than Jeannie Epper. "If I'm not working and hear about a major stunt being done, I go out to see how it's rigged," she says. "I want to know why that car doesn't do this or does do that. I want to know how much dynamite they put into an automobile to blow it up. I want to watch when they put a fire suit on, and see exactly how they get into it, and examine the inner wrap, and find out what protective gels are used." Why all that time invested in watching other stunt people? Because she wants to be sure she'll know what's needed if she's ever called on to do the same stunt. She wants to know everything the stunt coordinator knows, and more. It's all for her own protection.

"Stunt people must always search for the escape route," she adds. "If I walk into any room and there's only one door in it, I subconsciously know where that door is."

That's what planning is all about.

MOVIE STUNTS AND THE
PEOPLE WHO DO THEM

Helen Gibson in *The Midnight Express* from the "Hazards of Helen" series

The S. S. *Poseidon* is overwhelmed by a huge wave in *The Poseidon Adventure*.

Hal Needham leaping
from a moving airplane
(Courtesy Hal Needham)

Paul Stader taking
a fall from a horse
(Peter Gowland Photo)

Debbie Evans about to drive
through a burning barricade
(From the motion picture *The Jerk*.
Courtesy of Universal Pictures)

Bob Yerkes trains a young
stuntwoman on the trapeze
(Sandy Weiner)

Dar Robinson in *Highpoint*
(Photo by John Giannini and Alan Markfield)

Paul Mantz died during the filming of *The Flight of the Phoenix* when his plane crashed during the stunt.
(*The Flight of the Phoenix.* Courtesy of Twentieth Century-Fox. Copyright © 1966 Twentieth Century-Fox Film Corp.)

Two shots of Richard Epper during a winning performance in the horse event at the Hollywood Annual Stunt Competition
(Photos by Sandy Weiner)

The starting line as the gun goes off
for the motorcycle race at the Hollywood
Annual Stunt Competition
(Sandy Weiner)

Richard Epper demonstrating
his motorcycle skills
(Sandy Weiner)

A special-effects man prepares a car to explode. Ronnie Rondell drove the exploding car during the finale at the Hollywood Annual Stunt Competition.

(All photos by Sandy Weiner)

The fire crew rushes in
to help Rondell out of the car.

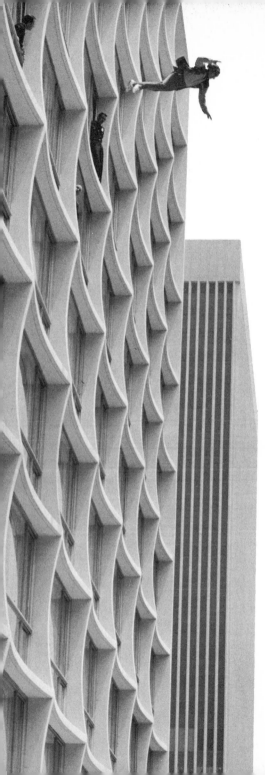

Terry Leonard in
an eight-story fall
(Jan Carpenter Leonard)

Paul Stader crashing through a window
designed to break away on impact (BELOW)
and (OPPOSITE) being knocked off a bridge
(Peter Gowland Photos)

Fire breaks out in the world's tallest building in *The Towering Inferno*.
(Courtesy of Twentieth Century-Fox. Copyright © 1974 Twentieth Century-Fox Film Corp. & Warner Brothers Inc.)

Two scenes from *The Towering Inferno*

A man on fire staggers
out of a burning elevator.
He is protected
by a fire suit.

Another man is forced
through the skyscraper's
window by the impact of
the water used to fight
the blaze.

Terry Leonard's fire stunt in *Apocalypse Now*
(Jan Carpenter Leonard)

Terry Leonard is helped
into the fire suit he
designed for this stunt.

Leonard on fire.

Curtis Epper (INSET), one of the youngest stuntmen
(Courtesy Jeannie Epper)

Epper practicing a fall
(Joan Adlen)

Hal Needham (INSET)
and performing a boat jump
(Courtesy Hal Needham)

Jeannie Epper (LEFT) doubles for Linda Carter as Wonder Woman on the television series.
(Courtesy Jeannie Epper)

Jeannie Epper in a car-hit gag
(Joan Adlen)

Debbie Evans performing
a dangerous car roll
(Jack Carpenter)

Kitty O'Neil
(Courtesy Kitty O'Neil.
Photo by Chuck Duncan)

Kitty O'Neil, the first female member
of Stunts Unlimited, doing a fire gag
(Courtesy Kitty O'Neil, Stuntmasters, Inc.)

KILLER STUNTS

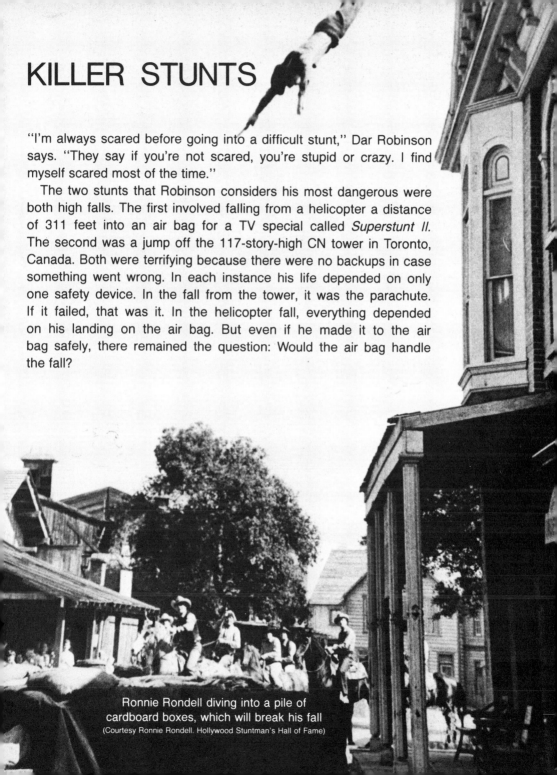

"I'm always scared before going into a difficult stunt," Dar Robinson says. "They say if you're not scared, you're stupid or crazy. I find myself scared most of the time."

The two stunts that Robinson considers his most dangerous were both high falls. The first involved falling from a helicopter a distance of 311 feet into an air bag for a TV special called *Superstunt II*. The second was a jump off the 117-story-high CN tower in Toronto, Canada. Both were terrifying because there were no backups in case something went wrong. In each instance his life depended on only one safety device. In the fall from the tower, it was the parachute. If it failed, that was it. In the helicopter fall, everything depended on his landing on the air bag. But even if he made it to the air bag safely, there remained the question: Would the air bag handle the fall?

Ronnie Rondell diving into a pile of
cardboard boxes, which will break his fall
(Courtesy Ronnie Rondell. Hollywood Stuntman's Hall of Fame)

Air bags come in various sizes, from 8 by 10 feet to giant bags of 50 by 100 by 25 feet deep. This last was used for the copter jump. Available only in recent years, these bags are blown up at the stunt site and act as pillows, releasing air as the body hits. Before air bags, cardboard boxes and mattresses of foam rubber, called Port-a-Pits, were often set up to cushion falls. Both are still in use, but for high falls, air bags provide the best protection. Still, from a height of 300 feet, the biggest air bag looks like a minimarshmallow.

It's possible to estimate the greatest height from which a fall can be made safely to an air bag. Still, estimates can be wrong.

A. J. Bakunis, a 27-year-old stunt man, is a case in point. Before his last jump he had made 2,500 successful jumps of over fifty feet.

During filming of the movie *Hooper,* A.J. jumped 232 feet from a helicopter into an air bag. This gained for him the world record for a high fall. From 1973 until A.J.'s jump in 1978, Dar Robinson had held that record.

A few months after A.J.'s record fall, Robinson regained the record with a 311-foot jump, also into an air bag. This prompted A.J. to plan a leap from the twenty-three-story Kincaid Towers in Lexington, Kentucky. The 323-foot fall would prove he could do it and survive and take back the world record.

On September 22, 1978, he carefully set up his canvas and plastic air bag. He was warned that it was too small and not strong enough, but A.J. had helped design that bag and believed in it.

When he jumped, his accuracy could not have been better. He landed dead center on target, falling at 80 to 82 miles an hour. But his body sliced through the bag like a knife through cake. The twelve-foot-high bag couldn't take the force of his fall. He hit the ground, bounced up, and hit again. The impact broke his hips and shoulders and destroyed his lungs. He lingered in a hospital for fifteen hours before he died.

Stunts vary in difficulty from the no-brain simple stair fall to the complex motorcycle leap involving an explosion. The latter takes engineering, skill, courage, and luck.

Dar Robinson tells about a motorcycle stunt he is planning, revealing just enough details to show that what looks easy on television or in the movies isn't. There are many secrets to setting up and performing a difficult stunt that the viewer doesn't see. Sometimes special equipment must be designed and tested. Testing with dummies often goes on; then, if the stunt fails, it's the dummy that blows up, not the stunt person.

The current world record for jumping a motorcycle from one ramp to another is 190 feet. On a live TV show Robinson will pretend to try bettering that record. He'll charge off a ramp at full speed. But instead of making it across the open space, about midway his motorcycle will explode. At this point, Robinson will fall to the ground, into an air bag between several cars.

Why is this stunt such a killer? Because the motorcycle will be hurtling forward at 80 mph at the moment it explodes. It would be normal for Robinson to be flung forward some distance before falling. However, he has designed special decelerating equipment. Precisely how it works he won't say. But if all goes well, this is what will happen: The motorcycle will blow up; Robinson will come to a complete stop; the motorcycle will keep going.

Stopped in midair by his decelerating device, Robinson will fall to the air bag set up below. But even a half second too late in timing, and he could be carried beyond the air bag. "You just have to know what you're doing in such a stunt," Robinson says. "This kind of thing can kill you."

One of the most dangerous stunts ever performed on a horse is Yakima Canutt's famous horse transfer. Canutt was a master at horse transfers. He could gallop close to a moving train or stagecoach. Keeping his speed and distance constant, he would transfer from the horse to the moving vehicle.

Canutt performed a stunt that people still talk about with wonder. In *Riders of the Dawn* (1938), when he doubled for Jack Randall, and again in *Sunset in Eldorado* (1943), he transferred to a fast-moving stagecoach while riding at full gallop. There he beat at the villain and was knocked off the coach to the backs of the horses pulling it. From there he fell between a pair of horses to the ground. As the coach passed over him, he seized the rear axle and was dragged some distance over the ground. Finally, he managed to climb onto the back of the coach, cross the roof, and dispose of the villain.

How could a man perform such a stunt and live? True, the camera may have undercranked, so the action looked faster on the screen than it really was. True, Canutt wore padding in important places. But still, he had to avoid the horses' hooves, be dragged over rough ground, and pull himself up from under the stagecoach wheels while the coach was speeding along. There was no trickery; Canutt did it just as we saw it. He figured out how it could be done and had the physical control and courage to do it.

Andy Epper describes what was for him the most frightening stunt. In 1974 he doubled for the phantom in *Phantom of the Paradise*. The stunt called for him to move very slowly by handholds along a curtain rod about forty feet above a stage. The camera was shooting down, so nothing could be set up on the stage to catch him if he fell. It would be seen.

Before attempting the stunt, he practiced close to the ground. He set up a forty-foot-long bar, the distance he would have to travel. If he fell from this practice bar, it would be only a few feet. After much practice, he was certain he could do the same thing from the curtain rod high above the stage.

During the filming he wore gloves, pulling his weight hand-by-hand across the bar. About twenty-five feet along the forty-foot length, a problem developed. The gloves began to roll under his palms because he hadn't taped them well. With each new handhold the gloves rumpled more, making a knot of cloth in his palm. He could not get a firm grip. His heart began to pound, and sweat poured down his neck. The end of the rod looked a mile away. That hard floor forty feet below would break every bone in his body. He didn't think he could make it. Unable to hold on one more second, he made a last, frantic grab for the hold which would put him on solid ground. Panting and drained, he barely made it.

The scariest stunt for Jeannie Epper came while doing the film *1941.* The story is a spoof of the Pearl Harbor attack. It takes place in California. "This guy freaks out," Jeannie says, "and thinks he sees all the Japanese invading. He gets a big old cannon and doesn't know how to shoot it, so he blows off part of his house. His wife is trying to get everything out of the house. She opens the front door and sees him coming at her in a tank. She slams the door shut and runs for her life as the tank rolls through."

Jeannie doubled for the wife at the door. A heavy cable was supposed to stop the tank right at the door. Jeannie was expected to open the door and shut it just before the tank was stopped by the cable. That's all the camera would record in one take. A second shot would show the tank rumbling through the house, but by then Jeannie would be safely out of the way.

In the first take Jeannie opened the door, saw the tank almost on her, slammed the door, and ran. The second take she also ran, but seeing the cable hold the tank, she wasn't quite as frightened as before. By the sixth take Jeannie had come to trust the cable. This time, when she shut the door, she just stood there. On that take, however, the cable snapped. Someone shouted a warning, but by then the tank was rumbling through. Some instinct alerted Jeannie. She jumped for safety just in time.

Sometimes, routine stunts turn out to be killers. Polly Berson, stunt woman for twenty-seven years, who doubled for stars such as Barbara Stanwyck and Anne Baxter, retired after one very dangerous stunt. It was in the Universal film *Earthquake.* There is a scene in which a man and woman run from a house as raging floodwaters roar down on them from a broken dam. Thousands of gallons of water struck Polly, who played the woman. The water pushed the man out of danger. But Polly was pinned against the wall of the house by the water and tossed and knocked about by the porch planking and other debris. Finally, she was trapped underwater.

Stunt people do get hurt and sometimes killed in their work. In the last five years five stunt men have died.

A. J. Bakunis's death, already mentioned, was caused by a poorly constructed air bag for the height of the fall.

Vic Rivers jumped a truck into a lake. The ramp he drove off collapsed as he drove up it. This caused his truck to enter the water differently from what was expected. Rivers had been told, had been *warned* to carry an air supply with him in case he went under. He didn't. When divers went down to find him, the truck was empty. He had managed to work free but had drowned because he hadn't carried an air supply with him.

Cap Parkinson, a very bright stunt man, lost his life in an unfortunate accident. He was sitting in the window of a car, steadying a camera, as the car raced forward. The vehicle blew a tire, rolled over, and cut him in half. His death could have been avoided, other stunt men say. He should have tied the camera down and not sat in the window.

The fourth stunt man to lose his life was Jimmy Shepard. His death came about while he was doing a stirrup drag stunt. In the film, he was supposed to fall from his horse and be dragged along the ground, caught in the stirrup. Because of all the noise of sound effects, guns shooting, and shouting, the horse spooked. It jumped, tossing Shepard around so that his head hit a hard-wood post. If Shepard had allowed himself a longer line instead of tying so close to the stirrup, he might have avoided the horse's hooves and the post.

The fifth man to die was performing a very difficult stunt. Still, if he hadn't been asked to repeat it one more time, he might still be alive.

For more than thirty years Paul Mantz had been a daredevil stunt pilot. He rarely turned down tough assignments. Director Robert Aldrich asked Mantz to use a plane purposely designed to look as if it could not fly and to make it fly—just barely. It was for the film *Flight of the Phoenix.* In a wild climactic scene, the *Phoenix* struggles into the air and manages to fly to civilization.

Mantz took off to do the stunt on a July morning but turned back when his engine overheated. The next day he coaxed the plane into the air again, several times dipping into a valley, touching his wheels down and making it out. When he landed, satisfied with how he handled the stunt, he learned he had been too close to the camera. Do it once more, he was told.

"Well, here we go again," Mantz said as he strapped on his cloth helmet. He flew over the dunes at about 100 feet. The tiny cockpit was so shallow that half of his body seemed to be sticking out in the open air. He made one pass. It was good. On his second pass he touched the *Phoenix* down twice and barely missed some dunes. It was perfect. The directors radioed their congratulations. Then they asked him to do it just one more time, "for a protection shot."

It was about 6:45 A.M. by then. The valley was heating up fast. The heat currents would try to lift the *Phoenix* while Mantz tried to pull it down. The stunt man had sworn he'd not try this stunt any time the temperature built up too high. But he was anxious to get it over with. "Okay, one more time. That will be the last," he said.

It was. He made it back into the valley and touched down. He hit once, flew for about 100 feet, then hit again, bounced around, wheels breaking through the crusty sand. Again he wobbled into the air, trying to get the nose up and tail down. The plane began to break apart. The prop dug into the sand, and the fuselage began to somersault along the valley floor. Paul Mantz died in the sand. The finished film showed the grotesque *Phoenix* fighting its way into the air, rising over the sand dunes around the valley, and flying off to safety.

"It's usually not the hard stuff that gets you," Dar Robinson says. "Hard stuff you work out in advance, very carefully, and besides, not many people can do that kind of work anyway. It's the easy stuff that's dangerous." More than one stunt person says the same. When the stunt looks easy, watch out.

But it's clear from the experience of Paul Mantz that the hard stunts are killers, too.

HOLLYWOOD'S ANNUAL STUNT COMPETITION

Indian Dunes, California. September 1, 1979.

It's 6:00 A.M. For the last half hour motorcycles have been roaring into Indian Dunes a few miles from Magic Mountain. They are followed by motor homes and campers and vans carrying horses. By 6:10 the best spaces under the trees are taken. Both sides of the wide dirt path leading to the competition grounds are jammed with wheeled vehicles and horses tethered to nearby trees. Midway to the competition area the snack wagon is set up, and workmen hammer together a small grandstand. A rock group begins unloading its equipment, starts tuning up. From the vans comes the smell of coffee brewing, bacon frying, eggs sizzling.

By 7:00 A.M. folding chairs bloom beside each camper. It's visiting time. In the small world of stunt people everyone knows everyone else. Many have worked together. Some haven't seen their friends since the last film they did together. It's a family reunion: backslapping, handshakes, hugs, kisses, news traded eagerly.

Richard Epper, far left, during the motorcycle race at the Hollywood Annual Stunt Competition
(Sandy Weiner)

The CBS television crew has arrived. They unload miles of cable, microphones, cameras, vehicles with long extensions like firemen's ladders, on top of which cameramen will sit. Fire trucks and ambulances roll in to stand by.

At eight in the morning the sky is bright blue, the air still cool. Cars with parents and kids and even grandparents bump over the dusty road to the parking area. Some are friends of stunt people. Some have heard of the event on the radio. Some follow any sporting competition, especially ones involving danger, like the events today.

Only eight men and one woman will be competing in this fourth annual Hollywood Stunt Competition. The nine chosen were selected from a long list of hopefuls. They feel lucky to be here. This day shows off their talents. How they perform will be watched by the stunt coordinators who do the hiring. Future jobs will surely come from this day's events.

There will be three competitions—horse, motorcycle, and car. Each winner takes home a handsome Suzuki 400cc motorcycle. The one person who earns the highest overall performance score receives a check for $5,000 and a new automobile.

This is the day the Epper family have looked forward to for weeks. Richard, twenty-one, is one of the competitors. The entire family is out to root for him—grandma and grandpa Epper, mama Jeannie, and stepfather Lee Sanders, two aunts and three uncles, cousins, sister, and brother. Almost all are or have been stunt people.

Richard knows how fierce the competition will be. He'll be up against the very best of the younger stunters—Buddy Joe Hooker and Allen Gibbs, among others. Everyone knows them. They've even got fan clubs. People strut around wearing Allen Gibbs T-shirts. Girls wear jeans saying, "I'm for Buddy Joe." Still, Richard has his fan club, too. He is surrounded by his tight-knit family and a crowd of supportive friends.

The first event will be the horse race. It is held along a wide dry riverbed, flanked by healthy willow trees. But before the event cousin Johnny Hocks performs a stunt for the TV cameras. He gallops forward, then falls from his horse to be dragged along the ground, one foot still locked in a stirrup. At some point the strap holding his foot is supposed to release. It doesn't. He's dragged some thirty feet, head only inches from the horse's hind leg before someone runs in to stop the horse. Johnny stands. He's unhurt.

While the men and horses get ready for the race, the spectators sit on the bank of the dry riverbed and wait. Roy Quirk, wearing cowboy hat and boots, jeans, and plaid shirt, stands quietly by, watching. He raises horses and trains them for use in films now. When a scene calls for a herd of wild horses or a bucking bull to come snorting out of a chute, they may be his animals.

Roy didn't always raise horses. First, he worked in rodeos. Then he became a stunt man. One of only a few black stunt man, he specialized in westerns, doubling for James Garner, Dennis Weaver, and Sidney Poitier. "Not a bone in my body hasn't been broken at some time," he says. Then why did he stay in stunting so long? "No matter how scared you get, or how many bones you break, you do what you know how to do best," he says.

The Horse Event

The riders, on their mounts, line up, positions determined by their drawing lots. Richard, wearing a No. 10 on his shirt, will be in sixth position. He looks intent, but relaxed, as he waits for the sound of the starting gun.

The event demands that each rider race to a point about 200 feet from the starting line. Then he must make his horse fall to the ground. As soon as the animal has been brought down, the rider must race on foot to a fresh horse being held for him a few feet away. He must mount that horse and race along a trail which winds among the willow trees and over a creek to the finish point, about a mile. There he must dismount.

The gun fires. There's a flurry of movement. Sand kicked up by the nine horses blurs the scene. There seems to be a line of horses rearing up, then falling. Where is Richard? He's behind the line, apart from all the frantic cluster. He brings his horse down. On foot, he races between the chaos of men and fallen horses to mount the fresh horse. Then he kicks off and is gone. It's hard to follow him. The riders must circle the course twice. Everyone is yelling on his or her favorite, and dust is everywhere.

Then it's over. The first to cross the finish line is Lynn Glasgow. But wait! He's disqualified. He didn't bring his horse down. The win goes to the second man to come in. It's Richard Epper! His face is one big smile. His mother rushes in to hug him, and friends crowd around. Ken Squire brings him to the microphone, interviews him before the TV camera.

One event won. Two more to go.

Why did Richard win the horse event? Grandfather John Epper, Sr., says,

"Richard is a first-class horseman. He prepared himself well these last three weeks, like any good athlete. He trained his horse to run in the sand, kept a cool head, and had a good horse. He planned his strategy—to conserve his horse's energy in the first part of the race so the horse had that little extra needed in the last yards. Richard wanted to win and was totally prepared. That's what makes a good stunt man."

The crowd drifts away after the race, moves up the dirt path to the motorcycle race grounds. Indian Dunes serves as a motocross racetrack. It's one of the higher-speed tracks, a TT (treacherous track), not an FT (flat track). In the three-quarter mile, it has six good turns with three good high-speed jumps. The jumps follow one after the other, making the ride tricky.

The nine motorcyclists all start together, go into a straightaway, then over the jumps. They can collide or overshoot a turn after a fast straightaway. At times they may hit speeds of 90 mph, then ahead face a hairpin turn. They must throw their bikes into a 180, apply their emergency brakes. It's dangerous. Only motorcyclists who know what they're doing dare compete on such a course.

But before the race camera crews must move their equipment, lay out their lines of cable. Several hours will pass before this event. People go off to sit in the shade, to find refreshments.

Among the parked vehicles a special car stands out. Black, it hardly seems worthy of note at first. Men are working under its hood and inside its body. It's the warning sign in front that draws attention: "Danger! Explosives!"

This is the car being rigged for the final dramatic stunt after the competition. It will be driven only a short distance. At a set moment it will explode. The roof and doors will fly off. The car will burst into flames.

The man who will drive this special car, who will be inside when it explodes, is Ronnie Rondell. Twenty years a stunt man, he has doubled for Robert Blake and was stunt coordinator for *Baretta,* the TV show. He'll be wearing a fire suit, a crash helmet, earplugs, gloves, an oxygen tank. Restraining safety belts will protect him from whiplash.

The car Rondell will be driving, a test vehicle, almost new, was by Pontiac. After use in the stunt, no matter what its condition, it will be returned. Often Pontiac engineers attend stunt shows such as this to observe for themselves just how much punishment their cars can take.

Come close to the car. Outside, it appears to be normal. But inside, all

MOVIE STUNTS AND THE
PEOPLE WHO DO THEM

the guts have been removed. No soft seats. No soft padding on doors and ceiling. Just a bare shell. Bare? Hardly. In fact, the cabin is crowded with equipment.

Around the driver's seat stands a one-inch-thick Plexiglas wall. It forms a box in which Rondell will sit, sealed off from the exploding devices behind and to the side of him.

The plastic wall is the least of the innards. On the floor sit pots of black powder, cables attached to the doors, wires snaking busily from pots to boxes. The car has been rigged by special effects men, who know all about setting up for fire and explosion stunts. At the flip of a switch Rondell will set into motion a chain of explosions. The pot in the middle of the car will blow a hunk of cork up to the roof, popping it out. The roof has been precut, so it doesn't take much for it to separate. Each door is cabled off with a charge in the cables. When the charges go, the doors explode outward, restrained from flying into the crowd by twenty-foot-long cables.

Three lifters, or explosives, have been placed in the front, under the hood. Two lifters in back will blow off the trunk. The hood and trunk also have restraining cables to protect the crowd from being hurt.

Before Rondell takes off, a clunker box will be preset to a particular speed. When Rondell throws a switch on the dashboard, everything will blow fast, one after the other. Number one may be the back door, two the roof, three the hood, and so on. The car will burst into flames because only moments before he takes off, it will be painted with highly flammable rubber cement.

If all goes well, Rondell will be sitting in the car for about a minute after the explosions, with the car on fire. As soon as it's certain all bombs have gone off, the safety crew will rush in with fire extinguishers to get him out.

At this hour of the day, however, Rondell is not even near the car. He's off somewhere having a cold drink while his trusted crew, as careful as surgeons operating on a brain, measure and tape and lay wire inch by inch in the doomed car.

Motorcycle Event

At last, the motorcycle event is announced over the loudspeaker. First, there will be an eight-lap qualifying race. From those entering will come the fastest five. Only they may compete for the first-place title.

TV cameramen take positions along the raceway. Hundreds of spectators line the route, standing on cars and pickup trucks for better views.

The nine motorcyclists buzz into starting position. Their bikes shine like new. Even the spokes sparkle in the sun. Only different numbers on their shirts distinguish one helmeted rider from the next.

They're off! In a whirl of dust they spurt forward, each already struggling for the lead. The next minutes we see the riders pick up speed, sweep up the hills, fly off the hillcrests, bounce to the ground, and roar on to the next hill. They reach the curves, brake hard, bikes almost parallel with the ground as they make the turn. Around and around the course they charge while each driver's lap counter keeps score. A buzz-saw hum rips the air as motorcycles flash by. One gains on another. One falls behind. It's hard to keep track of the laps. But finally, the first man shoots past the checkered flag at the finish line . . . the second, third, fourth, and fifth.

The five who will compete for the race that counts are Buddy Joe Hooker, Allen Gibbs, Mick Rogers, Richard Epper, and a young woman—Dawn Grant. Last year Debbie Evans came in second in this event.

In this qualifying race Richard Epper took third. Not a good sign for someone wanting to take first place in the race ahead. Was he saving his bike or his concentration?

Now only five motorcyclists line up. The flag goes down, and heads low, they zoom into the straightaway. Again it's hard to count the laps, hard to judge who is pulling ahead. But finally, the word goes out. It's the final lap. Buddy Joe Hooker is in the lead. Richard, in second place, doesn't seem able to close the gap, to gain ground. There's just one more hill to negotiate, then a turn, and the straight race to the finish line.

Something happens. Hooker, perhaps sensing Epper close behind, hesitates or tries too hard. In that second he loses control. Richard, taking advantage, shoots by.

Epper is the winner a second time. The crowd whistles and shouts and screams. A newcomer, he's only a kid—twenty-one years old. Yet he's beaten the regulars, the big names. He seems stunned as his family and friends laugh and cry and hug each other. He seems unable to believe it's all happening to him.

The Epper family gathers to calculate Richard's chances of becoming the overall winner. With the car race next, he can afford to come in fourth and still be high-point winner. The pressure is off. Unless Richard really bombs, he's got the big win in his pocket.

The Car Event

Many people drive cars well. But the car race takes more than driving well. It takes stamina, nerve, and quick thinking, as well as know-how. Many race car drivers also race motorcycles. Many first learned on motorcycles. Expertise on the first translates to the second.

The cars used are all Trans Ams with 450 engines. They are identical, the same year models, and very fast.

There will be eight laps, just as for the motorcycle event. This time, however, the drivers stand behind and to the right of their vehicles. When the signal flag snaps down, each runs to his car, jumps in, starts the engine, and speeds off. The course is the same as for the motorcycles, along a straightaway, over three consecutive hills, around hairpin turns, eight times. No. 10 car belongs to Richard.

It's a grueling course. Dust flies back from the forward cars, clouding windshields, cutting visibility like a heavy fog for the cars behind. Because of the speed at which the hills are taken, the cars actually leap from the hilltops, wheels off the ground. They sail through the air to land with a jolt, wheels spinning for grip, before spurting forward toward the next hills.

These are the chariot racers of modern times. Wheel to wheel they challenge each other every yard of the way. It's a contest of the best for the title of champion.

The day is almost over. Sun has baked the course to a fine dust. The spectators look weary and sunburned. But this is the last event. It determines the overall point winner, the man or woman who will take home the big prizes.

It's Buddy Joe Hooker who sweeps through the finish line first. Not unexpectedly because Buddy Joe's reputation as a top car driver is well earned. Second in is Jerry Wills. While screams and yells shatter the air, eyes strain for the third car. It matters very much to the Eppers, who have been praying that Richard take third or fourth place.

He does!

Five minutes later a beaming Richard is being interviewed by CBS stunt show MC Ken Squire. Helmet in hand, Richard appears humble. Squire puts an arm around his shoulder.

For winning the horse event—a brand-new Suzuki motorcycle.

For winning the motorcycle event—a second, identical Suzuki.

For being overall point winner—a check for $5,000. A handsome silver trophy! And finally, a 1979 Trans Am car of his own.

The competitive events ended, there is still one more spectacular stunt for the spectators. Ronnie Rondell now dons his fire suit, gloves, and helmet. He climbs into the explosive-filled black car. A crew paints the car with highly inflammable rubber cement. Then Rondell starts up the doomed vehicle, picks up speed, and, when he's ready and at speed, flips the switch on the control box.

Suddenly this innocent-looking car driving over the dirt road explodes with a roar. The noise, though expected, shocks. Almost at once the roof flies off. The doors explode out. The hood and trunk flip up. Flames engulf the car. There is an awed silence.

Ronnie Rondell is inside that bombed car! *My God,* you think, *is he safe? Can they get him out?*

A fire squad rushes in with extinguishers. They rip open the door on the driver's side, pull Rondell out. He is in flames, too. Quickly the fire is extinguished. We breathe again. Rondell is safe.

So that's how it's done in the movies, you think. How many times have we seen the hero or villain drive off in just such a car. A few feet away the car suddenly explodes and bursts into flames. Surely whoever was driving that car must have died, we believe. But no. The camera films the actor-star getting into the car and driving away. Cut. The car explodes. Maybe the driver gets out, engulfed in flames. We believe it is the actor-star, but it isn't. A stunt man has performed the dangerous action the story calls for. The audience will never know his name. Although he has taken every precaution to assure his safety, sometimes it is not enough. Stunt work, no matter how well planned, is dangerous.

The fourth annual Hollywood Stunt Competition is over. The young champions who competed for prizes will be doubling for stars in the next year. They will be leaping over rocks and stream beds on horses, racing them and bringing them down. They will chase villains in cars and on motorcycles, pretending to be the policeman heroes whose parts they are playing for the moment. This competition has shown off their talents as stunt people.

MOVIE STUNTS AND THE
PEOPLE WHO DO THEM

THE EXPERTS
TELL HOW THEY DO IT

Stunt people must be varied. Just being a good motorcyclist isn't enough. It's not unusual for any one person to be expert with cars, on skis, in the water, on horses, and—incidentally, good at fights and stair falls, too.

Here's what some of Hollywood's stunt people say about what they do best.

Stair Falls

Falling down stairs isn't as easy as it seems. Although it's almost a "no brainer," there are more than a few tricks to doing it well.

Paul Stader performed a classic stair fall in a 1956 film called *The Boss*. He and two other men were handcuffed together at the top of a wide flight of marble steps. They were headed for prison, but

Yakima Canutt performs one of the most dangerous horse stunts ever done, his famous transfer from horse to stagecoach.
(Courtesy of Universal Pictures)

to prevent them from "spilling the beans," the bad guys arrive and machine-gun them. The men, riddled by make-believe bullets, tumble down the long flight of hard stairs.

Once the fall begins, there's little a stunt person can do to control himself. If the stairway is narrow, the feet and shoulders can be used to slow or direct the fall to some extent. But in the marble stairway fall the men just "went for it." Though padded in key places, "you get dinged in the hip, sore shoulders, elbows and knees," Paul Stader says. Being skilled at gymnastics helps teach you to fall well, but in a stair fall like that, tied to two other men, there's little control possible.

High Falls

High falls into air bags and using parachutes have already been mentioned. However, there are other kinds of high falls.

Paul Stader, a champion swimmer, has fallen many times into water. In *Hurricane,* he doubled for Jon Hall in a high dive from a cliff. A dive doesn't take you more than eight to ten feet deep, he says. The density of the water checks the fall.

When planning a high fall into water, Stader checks for obstacles, just as Terry Leonard did in *Apocalypse Now.* Stader wants to be sure he won't hit a rock or submerged reef. Also, tides affect water depth. What may be ten feet deep one hour of the day may be only five feet deep at another. Finally, Stader wants a safety man to stand by in case he gets into trouble.

"You always try to maintain body control during a fall," Gary Epper says. You learn this control being a gymnast. "You have to be aware, thinking all the time." Gary stunted in a TV show in which a fight took place on a rooftop. He took a punch which knocked him off the roof. But just as he was leaving the roof, he was bumped accidentally by another actor. Out of control, he hit a wall, which further threw him off balance. He had to keep a clear head and use all his gymnastic ability to bring his body back into position so it would hit the air bag on the ground some fifty feet below.

Knowing how to fall properly is essential. When testing an air ram for use in the movie *1941,* Gary was thrown ten times by the device, each time landing safely on the air bag. The eleventh time he was pitched not to the air bag, but to the ground. He landed on his shoulder, breaking his collarbone. But it could have been worse.

The air ram was later used in scenes in which a land mine explodes. As soon as a stunt man hit it, an explosion went off, and he was pitched into the air as if he had stepped on a real mine. The audience doesn't see that he landed on an air bag.

For this kind of testing Gary Epper was paid from $600 to $1,000 each time he stepped on the device. Fantastic pay, but he could have broken his neck. How much is a life worth?

For any fall you must know what you're doing. Even in small jumps of twenty to thirty feet, as Jeannie Epper has done many times on *Wonder Woman,* that's true. "You need intense concentration," she says. "Your body can't be turned wrong, or you may jab a knee in your face. You can tear your spine or break your back. We make it look easy. It's not."

Fights

In the first films, fight scenes were the real thing. Men really hit each other. Chairs were thrown; real glass windows, broken. Fractured jaws, black and blue eyes, and bruised shoulders were not uncommon until John Wayne and Yakima Canutt devised the pass-blow punch. It's a punch that doesn't connect with the body but appears to. The fist comes as far as a foot away from contact. At the instant the fist should hit, the person receiving the blow snaps his head back. It looks as if he received a punch when, in fact, he did not. The camera sees the punch going in, records the head snapping back, but never shows the actual contact. Most movie fights are done this way.

Gary Epper describes a fight he set up for the TV show *From Here to Eternity.* "You need to know what the script calls for. What emotions are the actors supposed to be feeling? Who will win the fight?" A fight is choreographed, just like a dance. "Each person involved knows what steps to take, what movements to make, what he should be feeling, so the end result looks genuine and exciting."

In *The Great Race,* there's a pie-throwing scene which continues for six minutes. Almost 100 people sling real pies at each other across a large room. At one point Natalie Wood takes a pie straight in the face. It may look easy, but this short scene took four days to film and involved 3,500 pies.

"My dancing career helped me be good at fight work," Jeannie Epper says. "It's interesting," she adds, "the public would rather see women fight than men."

Horses

In spite of one's expertise with horses, horse stunts still present enormous challenges in films.

The most difficult stunt *physically* ever done by Terry Leonard was on a horse. It was for a *Daniel Boone* TV show. The stunt was considered so simple it would normally have been given to an extra rather than a stunt man.

Leonard was called in to replace a stunt man who had *slipped and broken a leg in the bathtub.* He was expected to ride at a gallop as escort for a team-driven wagon. Sound simple?

It wasn't. During the scene, at a set moment, Indians ride out of the trees and attack the wagon. Leonard, using a new rifle which can shoot off five shots before reloading, must go into a gallop, turn in the saddle, lean backward to get his shots, and reload. All this must be accomplished while in camera range.

On the third shot, the horse bucked Leonard off because he was sitting in such an awkward position. What was supposed to be simple turned into a complex and difficult gag.

In *Little Big Man,* Hal Needham played an Indian trying to kill Dustin Hoffman. He had to jump from the stagecoach to the first of a six-up team of horses. Hoffman's double was on the horse alongside. The two men transferred to the next pair of horses, about fourteen feet away, and from there to the next set. All this time the horses were galloping at full speed. "If you missed," Needham said, "you were going to have a bunch of horses and a stagecoach running over you."

How is it done? It takes extraordinary horsemanship, perfect timing, physical agility, and great courage.

"You don't just say giddiyap, when you want a team of horses to work together," John Epper, Sr., says. "Handling four- and six-ups takes enormous skill. Few people today know the art. I'm teaching this to my grandchildren."

Stephanie Epper says the most difficult stunt she ever did involved a horse. She had to bring a horse over a five-foot jump and fall off at the peak of the jump. Aware of where she might fall, she asked that the camera be positioned out of her way and that soft sand be laid down on the ground where she expected to fall. She taped her ankles in advance for greater strength and wore padding. Her trampoline and tumbling experience helped in that fall, as in many others. "You learn how to land on your back and shoulders to minimize the hurt," she says.

"He's as tough as a Hollywood stunt man. . . ." That sentence refers to the old stunt men who did westerns. They were the toughest. One day they might go out and fall from the top of the saloon, the next ride a bucking horse, the next wreck a wagon. Much of their work was with horses, and horses, like people, are not predictable.

Car Stunts

Some of the most exciting screen footage shown in recent years involves car chases. Remember the scene in *The French Connection* with Gene Hackman careening around posts and into cars under the elevated trains? Can you imagine any police TV series that doesn't involve a car chase, often with a flip-over?

The people who double for stars in car stunts are not just good drivers. They are remarkable drivers. Even in their spare time they're out testing different kinds of cars under all kinds of conditions. What can and cannot be done with each vehicle? How far will a car roll after braking when you are driving at 50 mph, at 60 or 70? What does it take to make a Trans Am roll over?

When a film company plans a car chase, it may require tying off traffic on city streets for a few minutes while shooting. The driver handling the car must perform the called-for action the first time. Each repeat costs more money and disrupts the city's traffic system.

Some stunt people go to special schools for race car drivers. But most learn their driving in borrowed or rented cars.

Debbie Evans appeared in a recent *CHIPS* episode on TV involving a female car theft ring. In it she has to race the car around corners, then turn into a parking lot. There's a car in the way, and she appears to drive right over it, landing upside down a short distance away.

Debbie says a roll bar was inserted in the back of her car to prevent the top from completely flattening when it overturned. This was done to give her some headroom. She was strapped into the driver's seat, protected with a neck collar, and at impact bent sideways in the small space left between her head and the car roof.

Before attempting the stunt, Debbie practiced approaching the parked car many times. Each time she would swerve around a car, then line up to go up the ramp which was hidden behind the parked car. In the take Debbie would run up that ramp on two wheels. That would cause her car to flip over when it hit the ground in front of the parked car.

The camera was set up down the street, looking toward Debbie's approach. It did not see the ramp.

Debbie says she saw a few stars and got jarred around a bit doing this gag. But it was "all in a day's work."

Payment for car rolls varies. Hal Needham says, "If I'm asked to roll a car at forty-five mph, maybe I'll get a thousand dollars. But if I'm asked to roll the same car at ninety miles per hour and do a few other things, the charge could be twenty-five thousand dollars."

Fire

Fire gags are always done in cooperation with the special effects department of a film company. The stunt person often must rely on these people to know how much explosive to set to create the effect and the kind of fire suit to wear. Many stunt people are becoming expert in setting up such gags themselves as double protection for their safety.

In *The Towering Inferno* stunt coordinator Paul Stader worked with fire much of the time. In one scene, Mike Johnson emerged on fire from an elevator. A fan set at high speed was used to blow the flames back to protect Johnson's face. The viewer doesn't notice that he was wearing a bulky fire suit because the entire suit was ablaze.

Johnson performed one of the most difficult fire stunts in that film. Doubling for Bob Wagner, he had to run through a burning hallway holding his breath. The scene was filmed in several takes. "We'd have him go from Point A to B, then put out the fire on him and give him a chance to get a breath. Then he'd go from B to C and be put out again," Stader says. The gas jets causing the fire were adjusted up and down as Johnson went by, lower as he approached, higher as soon as he passed through. He wore a complete fireproof suit made of Nomex (which racetrack drivers wear), including several suits of Nomex underwear. Around his head he wore a big wet towel.

One of the screen's most dramatic fire scenes appears in *Apocalypse Now*. How carefully it was planned is described by Terry Leonard, stunt coordinator for the film.

"The scene involved the takeover of Charlie's Point in Viet Nam. Helicopters land, and ground soldiers swarm out to take over the village. One guy machine-guns a bunch of water jugs. One jug is booby-trapped, blows up, and takes off his leg. At this point the camera cuts to Robert Duvall, who says, 'I want my injured men out of here. Now!' "

A medivac helicopter comes down between palm trees to pick up the injured soldier. Meanwhile, two of the village elders, a man and woman, are herded to the helicopter. They are suspected of knowing who set the booby trap and will be taken back to Saigon for questioning. The chopper pilot wants to get going. It's dangerous staying on the ground for more than a few moments. The old couple are just about to be thrown into the copter when a young woman pushes through the soldiers. She grabs the man and woman and tosses a grenade into the rising chopper.

Nine feet off the ground the grenade explodes. The chopper bursts into flames (as if jet fuel had caught fire) and falls. Three crewmen are either blown out or stumble out of the burning chopper, engulfed in flames.

The scene might have been filmed in two takes. In one, the helicopter, carrying dummies, would explode and fall to the ground. Firemen would put out the fire. Then the stuntmen would get into the helicopter, and the fire would be reset. The second scene would show the men stumbling out in flames.

Leonard wanted to make the scene appear completely realistic. That meant no dummies, no two takes. He wanted to do the entire scene in one take, using live people.

There was much to consider before doing this stunt.

On rigging the chopper: How much explosive was needed to blow it up without overkill? What if the primer cord didn't explode right? Taped around corners, it tended to crimp. If it didn't burn right, it could land the helicopter upside down. The men inside would be trapped.

The nine-foot fall had to be considered. Each of the stunt men would be grasping hold bars during the jarring fall. If a handhold broke loose, where would the stunt man's arm likely land? Leonard examined the positioning of each brace, each rivet which might be in the way. Even the seat padding was designed to minimize back injury.

On rigging the men: Sometime before the crew went into shooting, Leonard visited Simpson Safety Equipment in Hollywood. The company builds drag race safety chutes and flame suits used in Indianapolis car racing. Leonard wanted a special thin fire suit designed. The usual full fire suit is so heavily padded that the wearer moves like King Kong. Simpson built special small air bottles and full face plates. The finished suit gave the stunt man more freedom to move naturally while giving as much protection as before.

On training the safety crew: Leonard personally could check and recheck the chopper rigging. He helped design and check out the fire suits. But one thing he could not fully control—the behavior of the safety crew.

Two safety men had to be trained for each of the three crewmen who would be in flames. "If fire burns even a small hole in any of the fire suits," they were told, "the men inside will boil like lobsters." The reason was simple. The air temperature outside was 105 degrees with 99 percent humidity. The men in the suits were sweating. Fire would heat that sweat into steam. In two seconds they could actually fry.

These were not known safety men. They were extras, former servicemen, trained to watch for trouble signals from each stunt man. They were instructed to give the cameras time to get their shots as the stunt men fell out of the helicopter. Then they were to rush in with their fire extinguishers.

When the scene was finally shot, everything went just as planned. On cue, soldiers and Vietnamese crowd around the chopper, the grenade is lobbed in, the chopper rises, explodes, falls, and the three men leap out, engulfed in flames.

Everything went perfectly, except all the safety men rushed to the first man to signal he was in trouble. Leonard signaled frantically that he was getting too hot. Finally, his safety men broke away and rushed to his side to put him out.

Knowing how a stunt is planned and executed tells much about these experts. What comes across most clearly are the traits they seem to share.

They are all agile people. In top physical form, they are as graceful as dancers, with the finest sense of timing.

They are careful people. Each action is planned meticulously. No gag is ever attempted when the stunt person feels unsure of its success.

They are people with great self-control, able to keep cool heads and improvise in any emergency.

They are people of great courage, for they know what the stakes are each time they perform a stunt. Still, they go out to meet new and more difficult challenges again and again.

Finally, they are people who love excitement. Even in their play hours they engage in what most people consider dangerous games.

GETTING
STARTED

Curtis Epper is a stunt man. He's only ten years old. He has doubled for a girl in dangerous action scenes on *Salvage I*, a TV series. In the film *1941*, he falls ten feet when the floor collapses, landing on a mattress on the floor below. Curtis is an excellent swimmer, ballplayer, horseman, and trampoline gymnast.

But how did a ten-year-old get to be a stunt man?

Debbie Evans is twenty-one. She's as comfortable on a motorcycle as most people are on their feet. This year she expects to earn $60,000 as a stunt woman. Not bad for a kid with only a high school education.

How did she become a stunt woman?

Jeannie Epper in a car-hit gag
(Joan Adlen)

Hal Needham was born in Tennessee, the son of a sharecropper. Today he's considered King of the Stunt men and is one of the most sought-after directors in Hollywood.

How did he make the amazing leap from hillbilly to the heights of Hollywood?

Kitty O'Neil is deaf. Has been since she was a baby. That doesn't stop her from being the world's fastest woman on wheels and one of the hottest stunt women today.

How did she get started?

How *do* people become stunt men and women?

Curtis Epper

Curtis was born into stunt work. He almost couldn't avoid getting into it. His grandfather, John Epper, Sr., now seventy-two, became a stunt man in the 1920s. How? He had come to Los Angeles from Switzerland, where his father was in the horse business. John Epper, Sr., was already an expert horseman before going to work for an uncle who owned a riding club in Beverly Hills.

One day Epper's uncle sent him to deliver a black horse to MGM studios. A stunt man was supposed to jump the horse over a Cadillac in which four Indians sat, wearing high silk hats. When the cameras rolled, the stunt man couldn't get his horse to jump. That was when Epper, then twenty-one, got his first job. The simple jump earned him $25, a great deal of money in those days. It was more than a week's pay for only a few minutes' work. He decided that this kind of work was for him.

Although the first job had come easily, it took awhile to get others. His big break came when he got the chance to double for Gary Cooper in a film. He worked as Cooper's or Ronald Reagan's double or in roles as cowboy or stagecoach driver or Indian for the next twenty-nine years. During those years he married and fathered six children.

John trained his three sons and three daughters in horsemanship, and soon they began getting work in films, too. Not many women could handle horses as the Epper girls could. When a scene required a woman who could drive a team of horses, one or another of the Epper girls was called.

Middle daughter Jeannie Epper Sanders, Curtis's mother, specializes in high falls and horse work and doubled on *Wonder Woman* for two of the twenty years she has been stunting. Curtis is the youngest Epper in stunt work. His sister Eurlyne, nineteen, brother Richard, twenty-one, cousins John, Jr., twenty-two, and Kim, eighteen, all followed in Grandpa's footsteps.

Curtis got his first job because he was part of the Epper family, well known in the stunt world. However, if he hadn't been good at what he did, there wouldn't have been a second job.

Debbie Evans

Not everyone can be *born* into a stunt family. Debbie Evans wasn't. Debbie, in fact, never even knew such work, which she considers "play," was possible—until one special day.

By the age of ten Debbie could run circles around most motorcycle riders. Her father had taught her everything he knew.

"Everything I ever did was stunt-related," Debbie says. "When I was a little kid, I could wheelie the farthest down the street. I rode a unicycle when I was eight. I competed with all the boys and usually won. When I was ten, my mother came home one day to find me hanging from the top of a lamppost."

Debbie lives for sports. She skis on both water and snow, skateboards, roller skates, rides horses, and plays racquetball. "Learn as many sports as possible—gymnastics, motorcycle riding, swimming—and learn to do them all well," she says to anyone interested in becoming a stunt person.

Debbie, at sixteen, had taken trophies for motorcycling at many national and international competitions. In 1978, at the age of nineteen, she entered one of the most demanding motorcycle events—the Scottish Six Day. Her trip to Scotland was funded by donors who responded to her appeal in a motorcycle magazine. The competition attracted 280 expert riders from all over the world. For eight hours on each of the six days they buzzed over logs, up rocky slopes, and down waterfalls. Scoring was based on covering the grueling course with the most expertise. At the end, Debbie placed 109th out of the 280 entered and came in 3rd in the 175cc motorcycle class.

Debbie's remarkable command of the motorcycle attracted lots of attention. Magazines began writing about her. This was a sport dominated by males. A female who could handle a motorcycle as well as a man made news.

Shortly after the Scottish Six Day success she answered the phone to hear an unfamiliar voice say, "Hello, Miss Evans. My name is Gene Hartline. How would you like to be in a movie?"

She could hardly believe it. Someone was offering to pay her, and pay her well, for doing on a motorcycle what she loved doing most and had always done for free before.

The movie was *Death Sport* with David Carridine and Claudia Jennings. The job offer, to double for Claudia Jennings in action scenes, made her eligible for membership in SAG, the Screen Actors' Guild. Without a SAG card, no actor can work in a picture.

For four months, on and off, she not only did all the motorcycle action but became one very eager student in this new exciting world. "How do they do a fire gag? Why do those bombs go off, and how? What do stunt people make for this or that?" she wanted to know. "It got so people were sick of answering my questions," she says.

In the two years since that first job Debbie has appeared in many movies and TV series. In a *CHIPS* episode she played the part of a car thief and drove a stolen car. To elude the police, she tore around corners, swerved into a parking lot, and flipped the car over. The car pancaked, but Debbie was just shaken. (See page 49 for how this was done.)

In the movie *The Jerk* Debbie drove a motorcycle through a wall of fire and was accidentally burned. (See page 14 for what went wrong.) In *1941* she took part in a big fight scene and wound up on the floor under four husky football-player types. In *Airplane* she played a bothersome Hare Krishna, pestering Robert Stack. The script called for Stack to give her a karate chop. "I can't hit a nice little girl like that!" Stack protested.

"But you gotta!" Debbie pleaded.

Reluctantly Stack swung his arm back just as Debbie flipped her head away. He didn't even touch Debbie, but on the screen it looks as if she took a nasty wallop.

Describing what she does, Debbie makes it sound as ordinary as taking a walk to the library. But there's a great degree of risk in even the simplest stunt. Recently a stunt man broke an ankle jumping from a six-foot rock.

Curtis Epper was born into a stunt family. Debbie Evans attracted the attention of filmmakers looking for a woman who knew motorcycles. Hal Needham lucked into his first job by happening to be in the right place at the right time.

Hal Needham

Needham was born in Tennessee but reared in Arkansas, Mississippi, Louisiana, and Missouri. A sharecropper's son, he grew up around horses and cattle. In his teen-age years he worked for circuses, where he learned how to handle cars and motorcycles in thrill shows. Then he went into the Air Force to serve during the Korean War. As a paratrooper he not only jumped from airplanes but tested parachutes for the military.

Once out of the service, he went to California and into a business as a tree topper. He became as agile as a monkey, scurrying up tall trees and balancing on narrow branches as he held heavy buzz saws.

While healing from a broken leg, he met a man who had done a few stunts on *You Asked for It.* Hal was very impressed. The man said, "You can do anything I did. Say, they're going to film *The Spirit of St. Louis* and need some wing walkers. You're good with planes. Want to try out with me?"

What was needed, the director said when Needham applied, was someone who could walk on an airplane's wing while in flight and do some parachute jumps. Not many people were as well qualified as Hal Needham to do that. He got the job.

He was now a stunt man with a SAG card. But for the next year he couldn't get another job. Older stunt men didn't want him around. He was competition. Finally, with only a few "nothing-type jobs" during that time, he decided to work as an extra. Studios hire extras for crowd scenes, for bodies in airports or barrooms, for scenes where people are needed for atmosphere. Needham figured that as an extra at least he'd be on a movie set. There, while hanging around, he'd watch what the cameras were doing and learn how things were done, and why.

While working on *Have Gun, Will Travel* one day, he got his chance. A scene called for several men to climb a tree. The stunt men hired couldn't do the climb well. Needham said, "I used to be a tree trimmer. Climbing trees was my business. Let me try." At first no one believed him, but when he put on a pair of climbing spurs and scrambled up the tree, he was hired immediately.

He did some four or five stunts for the Richard Boone show. Simple things, like "running and getting shot and falling off a rock about ten feet high, but nothing big." The TV people liked what he did, and he was asked back to play parts as an Indian falling off a horse or a cowboy, but nothing important.

Then Boone and his stunt man double had a disagreement. When the stunt man quit, Needham said, "Give me a chance. If I can do what you like, hire me. If you don't like what I do, you don't even have to pay me."

They gave him the chance, and for nearly six years Needham doubled for Boone in the series. His work consisted mostly of doing fancy horse mounts and falling out of stagecoaches and barn lofts.

It was the beginning of a career that took Needham a long way up the Hollywood ladder. For many years he doubled for Burt Reynolds, and in fact, Reynolds and Needham are very close friends. From a stunt man, he became stunt coordinator, a second-unit director (the person who directs all the action scenes), a writer, and now a director.

Kitty O'Neil

While Hal Needham got his first stunt job by being in the right place at the right time, Kitty O'Neil got hers because of her courage, remarkable ability, and personality.

Kitty became deaf when she was four months old, after an illness. Deafness hasn't stopped her from doing more than most women her age. She can read lips and does speak, although she's difficult to understand. Having never heard people talk, she can't know precisely how words sound.

"The most important lesson I learned from my parents was that there was no reason I couldn't participate in life to the fullest, even though I was deaf. They taught me not to feel sorry for myself. That's what I'd like to get across to others who are handicapped."

Kitty "drowned" for Lee Grant in *Airport '77,* was on fire in *Omen II,* and had a car careen over her head when it crashed through the window of a restaurant in *Foul Play.* She has appeared in many movies and TV series, including *The Bionic Woman, Wonder Woman, Baretta,* and *Police Woman.*

"I love doing dangerous things," she says. "Even as a child I used to ride my bicycle down the steepest hills as fast as I could. I'm never frightened because I keep myself in excellent physical condition and have faith in God."

From her earliest years Kitty loved sports, especially swimming. By the time she was twelve she was winning swimming and diving competitions. She succeeded in taking thirty-eight blue ribbons, seventeen first-place trophies, and thirty-one gold medals and became the AAU Junior Olympics diving champion. At sixteen her family moved from Texas to California. They wanted Kitty to train under former Olympic diving champion Dr. Sammy Lee. Dr. Lee trained her in three-meter springboard and ten-meter (thirty-three feet) platform diving for national and international meets. But when Kitty didn't make the diving team for the '64 Olympics in Tokyo, she turned to other sports.

Before long, she was into every kind of motor sport racing. Drag boats, top fuel dragsters, production sports cars, motorcycles, dune buggies, and snow-mobiles became her "toys." Almost any sport intrigued her: hang gliding, water skiing, scuba diving, sky diving, and many others.

In the next years she raced motorcycles in desert and motocross events, but she particularly loved the speeds she could go in specially designed cars. During recent years she's been competing against some of the world's greatest race car drivers—Parnelli Jones, Gary Gabelich, Bobby Ferro, and others, in off-road races such as the Mint 400, Mexican 1000, and Baja 500.

Other racers, some of whom were working also as stunt men in films, noticed Kitty. They were impressed with her unusual courage and "never-give-up" at-titude. Only five feet three inches and ninety-six pounds, she more than held her own with the big guys. Only Gary Gabelich had made better time than Kitty in a three-wheel vehicle. (Kitty clocked 618.324 mph, and Gary's record is 622 mph.) Kitty was breaking all kinds of world speed records on water as well as land.

"Ever think of working in films?" she was asked one day. "There aren't any women who can do the things you can, Kitty." The men who urged her to go in for stunt work belonged to Stunts Unlimited, a professional stunt men's club the thirty-seven members of which were tops in the business.

Her friends began training her, and news about Kitty's remarkable talents got around. She could do horse work, water work, high falls, car and motorcycle stunts, fire gags, fights—in fact, almost anything. Three years ago she got her first job with Universal Studios. Ever since she has been so busy she turns down calls. Stunts Unlimited elected Kitty the first female member of the organization.

About 200 men and women belong to the official organizations for stunt people in Los Angeles. Of those, fewer than 40 are women. Whether men or women, they all have the same qualities in common. All are physically fit. All are top athletes skilled at more than one sport. All show great courage and self-confidence. All perform, for excellent pay, the unusual action that is part of most movies today.

It's a small, select world of people and a hard one to break into. Knowing people who think you're good and will help you get your first job helps. But most of all, being tops at many kinds of sports is what it takes.

QUESTIONS
AND ANSWERS ABOUT
STUNTING

How well are stunt people paid?

The best earn more than $100,000 a year. Many, including women, earn at least $50,000 a year. The basic pay for a day's work is $225. Payment over that depends on the stunt.

How can I train for stunting
without attending a special school?

Do everything that involves athletics and coordination. Take up gymnastics and tumbling. Learn to ride a motorcycle, not just down the street, but in hard competition—in the desert, for example, where you must contend with all kinds of conditions. Learn to handle all kinds of cars, how to slide them and spin them. Become the best skier, swimmer, horseman. Take ballet lessons. Ballet develops strong legs, timing, and flow, essential to all stunt work.

Are there training schools for stunt people?

Yes, in California. A school in northern California trains race car drivers. At least two schools in southern California give basic training in stunting. However, these skills can be learned almost as well through activity in many sports.

What's the difference between stunting
and special effects?

Special effects people do the technical planning and work to create the unusual effect a writer or producer wants. They rig a car with explosives or other design features so it will flip over and pancake without hurting the stunt person inside when a script calls for that kind of action. They create artificial snow, make-believe blood, nondangerous explosions, floods, earthquakes, all kinds of disasters so that they look real on the screen. Often stunt people and special effects people work closely together because each must know what the other will do. If a special effects person rigs a wall to collapse, the stunt person wants to know when and how it will fall because it affects his safety and even his life.

What's a second-unit director?

A special director is often hired to direct the action sequences of a film. He is the second-unit director. He differs from the regular director in that he usually works not with the principal actors who speak the lines, but rather with their doubles, the stunt people who perform the falls, dives, jumps, fire gags, and car crashes that we think the principal actors are doing.

What chance has a newcomer
to break into the field?

Thousands of people inquire each year about getting into stunt work. There are few openings. The profession, many say, is already overcrowded, although there are probably no more than 200 working regularly.

Does that mean it's impossible to break in?

No. If you're tops at a variety of athletics, you might make it. It helps to know people in the business who can recommend you to those who do the hiring. It helps to hire on as an extra to see how films are made and be around in case a director needs someone for a special stunt that you can do. But be prepared to earn your living in other ways because it's very tough getting that first job.

Is stunt work really dangerous?

Yes. Hal Needham, now at the top of his profession, has been stunting for about twenty-five years. During that time he has broken forty-five bones and his back twice. He says he learned to work even when he was hurting badly. People do get hurt, and some even die.

What's the most dangerous stunt ever performed?

While many stunt people have answered that question in this book, Paul Stader says it best: "The most dangerous stunt I ever did? The next one."

INDEX